Under One Crown

A Renewed Look at Creation in Word and Image

Under One Crown

A Renewed Look at Creation in Word and Image

Written By
Raachel Nathan Jurovics
Sarah Stein
and
Mary Blocher

Illustrations By
Andrea Gomez

Published By
Under One Crown Publishing
2019

Copyright © 2019 Raachel Nathan Jurovics, Sarah Stein,
Andrea Gomez, and Mary Blocher

Illustrations copyright © 2019 by Andrea Gomez

All rights reserved.

No part of this book may be reproduced or transmitted in any form
or by any means without written permission from the publisher.

Book design by Scott H. Davis

Published by
Under One Crown Publishing LLC
Raleigh, North Carolina, U.S.A.
www.underonecrown.com
books@underonecrown.com

ISBN 978-1-7333732-2-7

Kavannah

An Intentionality for Contemplating New Possibility

Resh Lakish said, "There are seven heavens. . . . In the one called 'sky,' sun, moon, stars, and constellations are set." Here the sky symbolizes Yesod, through which the divine male and female, symbolized by sun and moon, unite.

—Babylonian Talmud, Tractate Chagigah 12b

Contents

Black Fire / White Fire   9

Artist's Introduction   13

Before the Beginning   19

Chullin 60b in Two Voices   29

Notes   59

Black Fire / White Fire

Rabbi Raachel Jurovics
Rosh Chodesh Tishri 5780 / September 29, 2019

I've long been enchanted by an ancient metaphor explaining the interplay between the black-letter text of Torah and the lived experience that informs Oral Torah: one is black fire, the other white fire. The black-letter text represents the imprint of revelation; the white spaces between letters represent an ongoing conversation between the fixed and the infinite.

Both forms resist the static. Black-letter text represents a jumping-off point for infinite interpretive potential, as it lacks vowels and punctuation, inviting constant re-evaluation and deepening spiritual insight. In the white spaces reside the unwritten, often startling understandings of those whose voices wait to be recognized as we move through seemingly linear time.

One might say that the vibrancy of the black-fire text depends on the ever-new voices manifesting out of the white fire. To my mind, Judaism may best be understood as an interpretive tradition, seeding growth with every insight arising from the interaction of text and interpretation. Out of this, we derive both *midrash*—spiritual re/interpretation of text—and *halacha*—the unfolding of Jewish law, accountable to ancient intention and contemporary ethical insight.

Over time, my studies drew me to question the simultaneous elevation and diminution of the sacred feminine and the "lived feminine" of women's experience. Repeatedly, I encountered the contrast of the Divine Feminine as the Source, Nurturer, and Distributor of All alongside the exclusion of women from traditional Jewish ritual practice and from the recorded voices of revelation and interpretation. How, I wondered, could our theologies (especially mystical theologies) assert both the essential power of the feminine aspects of Divinity and also put forward so many depictions of the *Shekhinah* as the weakened, besmirched, humiliated and separated partner of the Holy Blessed One?

My colleague, Professor Sarah Stein, and I explored the powerful consequences of the spiritually-grounded lessening of the value of the feminine, of the female. We wrote about its pernicious effects within the Jewish world and beyond, and we looked for an interpretive strand to loosen the hold of the teaching that the feminine needed repair in order to achieve its ultimate fullness of meaning.

Eventually, we focused attention on a foundational text, one that repeatedly appeared as explanation, justification, and root cause of the diminished Divine and human feminine. In Genesis 1:16, we read "So God made the two big lights, the big light to rule by day and the small light to rule the night, and the stars." Commentary found in *Babylonian Talmud Tractate Chullin* 60b refers to this Torah verse to explain the differential power of masculine and feminine, and it is the *Chullin* interpretation that we have re-imagined in *Under One Crown*.

In conversation around this puzzle, Mary Blocher led us to the strand we have followed—the way the adjectives "great" and "small" may be understood as expressions of variable power and influence, not as definitive distinctions between entities, between the Sun and the Moon: in other words, size doesn't correlate with power.

As Sarah, Mary and I began exploring how to expand this insight, we invited Andrea Gomez to bring her artist's vision into the process, as we knew the re-interpretation we were teasing out held potential for profound and moving visual expression. Thus, throughout the writing process, we have been in conversation not only with the black-letter text, but also with the imagery springing from the white spaces onto the canvases before us.

We invite you, too, as you engage with the following pages, to reconsider Genesis 1:16 as an invitation to mutually supportive, interactive, eternally cooperative action in our world by the energies known as masculine and feminine, and of their manifestations in the roles of Sun and Moon.

Artist's Introduction
Andrea Gomez
Rosh Chodesh Tishri 5780 / September 29, 2019

Book illustration is deceptively complex. The writer produces a body of work filled with narrative, metaphor, symbolism, characters and other complexities; in short, an entire mini-universe. The artist needs to occupy that world, understand it, and then leave it for a parallel universe. The task is not to simply make pictures of the writer's work, merely replicating the words in images. This would be redundant, perfunctory. Instead, a good illustrator wants to visually expand and interpret the literary material. So the illustrator walks a tension line between the writer's vision and her own, but with the goal of melding both into a symbiotic whole.

I am not an illustrator. When my writer/rabbi friends and colleagues asked me to illustrate their work, in fact to be witness to the process of conceiving the narrative, I declined. Repeatedly. For the past nearly thirty years I've been a painter and before that an animator. It was like asking a hip hopper to dance flamenco; both dance, but with totally different technique and dance forms. I felt unqualified.

In the end, I accepted, but not just due to my colleagues' persistence and faith in me. Although my careers as an animator and painter seem unrelated, there were unifying aspects. I have always been interested in non-verbal narrative and frequently studied all forms of illustration, contemporaneous and historical. I've had a life-long attraction to the Creation stories of Genesis that began as a child and that seems to surface in my work every decade or so. My work explores a wide variety of materials which may make a viewer wonder if the same artist is responsible for everything I've done, yet it is unified by a constant vision of movement, storytelling, color, line and visual tension.

So with this background, I began the thinking stage about the illustration of this *midrash* which ended up lasting a year. I had no formal religious education. I was approaching this material as an empty slate. I set about learning the calligraphy of the Hebrew alphabet, and I looked at various historical codex forms and narrative paintings from the thirteenth century to contemporary art. There were a thousand ideas, no direction. By the end of this period, my mind was filled with white noise, with no clue as to where to begin. Long days were spent merely sitting in my studio, frustrated and utterly discouraged.

Finally, there was a thread, a small opening, and the more I tugged at it, the more the confusion unraveled. The idea of Creation formed with the three Hebrew letters in YHVH (Yud-Heh-Vav), the representation of God's name, was a key. Each letter became an abstract form and exhibited an idiosyncratic character.

I imagined the absolute quiet of the void and the first letter followed by the others, over and over again, until they dissolved into lines, planes, particles and reformed into Creation.

Likewise, the form of the book became a rhythmic unrolling of narrative, the words in black and white line flowing into a color realization of the content, paragraph by paragraph, like a visual *niggun,* a wordless melody. None of these images was the product of my intentional thinking. The best ones merely flowed. In the end, all the forms imagined were built from the initial thread. The last image became the unifier: the fracturing of light culminating in a vision of the Tree of Life.

Before the Beginning

GOD'S PRIMORDIAL CREATIVE PARADIGM is Torah herself, the womb of divine Wisdom, birthing the genesis and the continued unfolding of our world:

"The Torah says, 'I was the artist's tool of the Holy Blessed One.' In the usual way of the world, when a king builds a palace, he does not build it out of his own mind, but he has an artisan, and the artisan does not build it out of his own mind, rather he has plans and diagrams, so as to know how he is to make the rooms and how he is to make the passageways. So, too, the Holy Blessed One looked into the Torah and created the world, and the Torah said, 'In the beginning, God created . . . ,' and there is no 'beginning' but Torah, as we read, 'The Eternal created me, the beginning of God's path'" (Proverbs 8:2).

As the paradigm of paradigms, Torah presents herself to us as a manifestation of divine potential—infinitely more potential than any of the paradigms by which human minds impose order on the reality we experience. With every return to Torah, the source paradigm of being, we have an opportunity to discover alternative understandings of the content and meaning of our universe and its inhabitants.

Elsewhere in the Book of Proverbs we find: "*sh'ma b'ni mussar avicha, v'al titosh torat imecha*, Listen, my child, to the instructions of your father, and do not forsake the Torah of your mother" (1:8). While most voices recorded in our textual traditions have been male, sacred instruction comes to us in a chorus of voices, masculine, feminine, and non-gendered alike, in accord with Torah's primordial paradigm.

Thus, we engage Torah along with Beruriah, Dulcie of Worms, Malkah of Belz, and Hannah Rachel Werbermacher of Ludomir. We learn Oral Torah from the indwelling divine presence, the *Shekhinah* Herself. In our deep listening, all voices can be heard, not only in a female/male binary but also in the breath-spaces between words, in turns of phrase or intellectual leaps, in the heart-dance of ecstatic insight.

Torah poses infinite questions. For example: "So God made the two big lights, the big light to rule by day and the small light to rule the night, and the stars" (Genesis 1:16). We start with two big lights, and, on the other side of a white space with hardly room enough for a breath, we find one big and one small light. What happens in the white space between the two parts of this verse?

A POWERFUL STRAND in Jewish mystical tradition understands the evil we experience as a consequence of what transpires in that white space. According to some *midrash*, the dark side of the Moon serves as "the metaphysical breeding ground for all the impure forces in the universe, . . . the very root of evil and the font of its continued nurture from that point on."

Indeed, according to this influential interpretive motif, God's design for the universe requires the Moon's diminishment in order to account for evil and suffering. Some interpreters correlate the diminished Moon—plainly associated with the female archetype—with the very paradox of theodicy (the struggle to explain the origin of evil): how do evil and suffering find a place in a universe created by a good and omnipotent God?

God responds by claiming responsibility for the fullness of reality—a fullness beyond gendering. For example, in mystical understanding, the Torah verse "*ein ohd milvado*" implies not only that there is *only* one God, but that there is *no-thing* besides God. Elsewhere, God asserts: "I form light and create darkness; I create *shalom* (wholeness, wellbeing) and I fashion evil (what we experience as woe)." Thus, as corollary to divine responsibility for the entirety of reality, divine will requires that everything be possible, even that which we experience as evil.

All sacred stories, including some of the *midrashim* and commentaries explaining the reduced size and brightness of the Moon, invite us to explore Divinity's revelation of its deepest self. We are challenged in this exploration by a foundational text, *Tractate Chullin* 60b in the Babylonian Talmud, which has been predominantly understood as pointing to the feminine archetype as a source of evil.

It is not that the early rabbis cited in the *Chullin* text intend to set us on a "wrong path," rather that the text expresses and reinforces a narrative of hierarchy and diminishment, a narrative that reflects sociological realities in tension with the more egalitarian spiritual teachings we need to bring to the fore in our day.

No matter the sophistication of mystical teaching, which carefully distinguishes between archetypes and individual human beings. No matter that God creates the first human being male and female, female and male equally expressive of God's own image. In practice, when we assign all that we experience as evil or suffering to the feminine, we undermine the spiritual equality of masculine and feminine and disadvantage women (along with non-heterosexual male identities) in all aspects of life. We undermine the potential for a wholesome, redemptive collaboration of female and male capacities, however expressed, as equals.

WHENEVER WE UNDERMINE the human feminine, we undermine the divine feminine. The images we hold of God tend to reflect our still patriarchal social structures and their definitions of the relative nature of masculine and feminine.

Even when we claim to be alluding to qualities distributed among men and women regardless of sex, we still act on our perception of differing human natures based on appearance and physiology. When "woman" becomes shorthand for evil and suffering, women and the feminine—whether expressed in the flesh or in the divine spirit—endure lower stature, lessened respect, and damaging blame and guilt.

This form of theodicy bolsters a mythology that works backward from patriarchal reality. This distorted perception distracts us from other ways evil and suffering may be accounted for without assigning sole responsibility to the feminine. If, indeed, all qualities that reside within Divinity replicate within individual males and females regardless of physical form, then alternative explanations can surely be imagined.

The problem lies not with Jewish literary tradition, which has always been multi-vocal and which embraces all expressions of divine nature as equally holy. Indeed, the tradition includes nuanced alternatives to *Chullin* 60b that open up less hierarchical understandings of the interplay of masculine and feminine potentialities within the Divine.

The problem, rather, resides in the short-hand of human storytelling, in the narratives of dominant Jewish myths—myths that often favor sociological influences over the theological principles of faith—in which the feminine (including the Divine Feminine) has come to be viewed as lesser, as impure, as needing restoration.

If we accept the equality of feminine and masculine, we accept the obligation to listen for different responses to the inescapable question: How can evil derive from the same Source as good? If evil and good alike derive from the Divine, from what aspect of Divinity do they come?

Every interpretive choice both seeds and constrains future interpretation, so the first step in an interpretive process matters profoundly. In our day, with the renewed (and renewing) impulse to honor all aspects of Divinity, we seek to respond differently to the holy question set forth in *Chullin* 60b. We seek to investigate alternative paradigms of creation's content and meaning.

For example, we may ask ourselves, "What might be revealed if we start the narrative about Sun and Moon from a non-hierarchical perspective, assigning each a role of equal power?" If we choose a different beginning, how might our subsequent interpretations differ?

IN EVERY GENERATION, we are blessed with new voices to attend to, speaking Torah from out of the holy white space where the two big lights were transformed in response to *tzorech ga'voha*, a divine necessity. What follows represents one alternative possibility of many, an alternative derived from Torah's infinite storehouse of divine paradigms.

In your reading, perhaps you will find inspiration for yet another strand of *midrashic* response to *Chullin* 60b. Perhaps you will be among those who lead us to a transformative renewal of sacred language, liturgy, and wisdom to express the Unity of our One Source. Perhaps you will discern how our tradition might grow into new potential if female and male begin with equal power.

Now then, listen carefully to *mussar avinu*, the instruction of our Father voiced in one influential ancient text, and to *torat imeinu*, the Torah of our Mother guiding us to new insight.

Chullin 60b in Two Voices

MUSSAR AVINU (Instruction of our Father):

Rabbi Shim'on ben Pazi pitted one against another: "God made the two big lights" and "the big light [to rule by day] and the small light [to rule the night, and the stars]."

TORAT IMEINU (Torah of our Mother):

Mai "gadol"? How are we to understand "big"?

Before the lights were set in the firmament, "*va'yehi erev, va'yehi vokeir*, there was evening, and there was morning—a complete day" (Genesis 1:5b). The Creator's design required the life-giving properties of both night and day.

Prior to creating the celestial lights, the Divine Will looked into Torah and saw in the unfolding of time an alternation of evening and morning. Earth-time would require two great lights, a steadfast center—the Sun—and the fertile certainty of change—the Moon.

Just so, at the impossibly subtle boundary of dark and light, the Divine Will set a life-giving tension: an endless yearning linked the Sun—a bright stillness around which the planets orbit—and the Moon—her visible size ever transforming in the Earth's night sky, ever phasing through cyclic reflections of sunlight. Both heavenly lights are big in meaning, both are great in purpose.

Mussar Avinu:

The Moon said before the Blessed Holy One: "Master of the World! Is it possible for two rulers to govern under the same crown?" God said to her: "Go and make yourself smaller!"

Torat Imeinu:

"Master of the World! It *is* possible for two rulers to govern under the same Crown, the Crown beneath which every form of being in all its created diversity reveals your boundless power. The Crown sits above the other emanations of Divinity and sets the role of each aspect of Being throughout eternity.

"Partner me with my beloved, the Sun, and I will nurture the boundless potential for life and transformation on Your Earth. As the light of the Sun bursts forth, daytime life will flourish. Without respite from its glare, however, some life forms will wither under punishing heat. In the modulation between the Sun's light and mine, we will fulfill your Will that every possible form of life take root in your world.

"Receiving and reflecting the Sun's rays, I rule the cradle of darkness. Under my gentle, cycling light, your world will take respite. Night creatures will feed, seeds grow. At the darkest point of my monthly passage, death itself will move back into life—from *gilgul* to *gilgul,* cycle to cycle, life always changing, yet never diminishing."

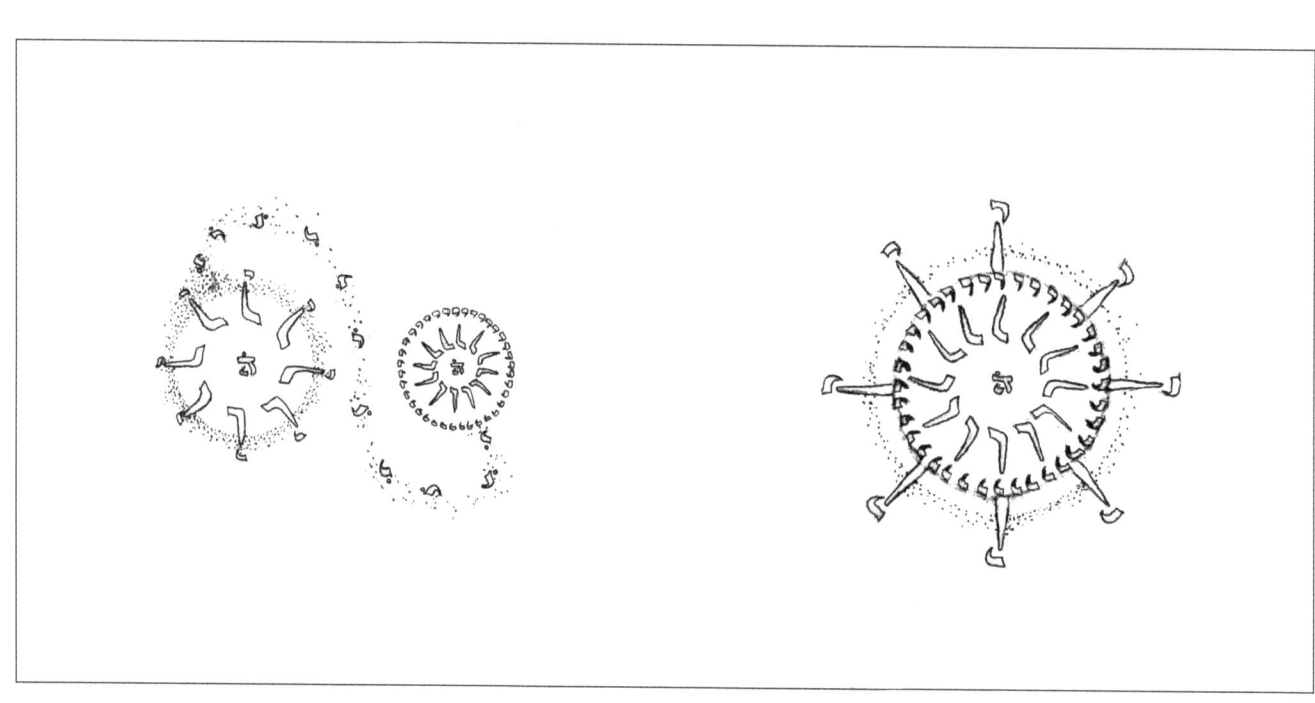

Mussar Avinu:

She said before God: "Ruler of the World! Because I said something reasonable before You, am I to make myself smaller?" God said to her: "Go and rule by day and by night." She replied: "What importance does that have? What use is a lamp in daylight?"

Torat Imeinu:

And God said: "In daytime, the Sun's radiance will outshine your pale reflected light, yet your presence will be noted. Your regular waxing and waning will remind all life on Earth that Sun and Moon govern together under the Crown of Heaven."

The Moon replied: "The Sun and I ever serve You in unity. There is evening, and there is morning, and in our twice-daily reunions at the boundary point, together we resolve every separation, every exile. At our every return, Divine Giving and Receiving embrace before the Throne of Glory. And the heavens declare: *Adonai Echad u'Sh'mo Echad,* YHVH is One and God's Name is One" (Deuteronomy 6:4).

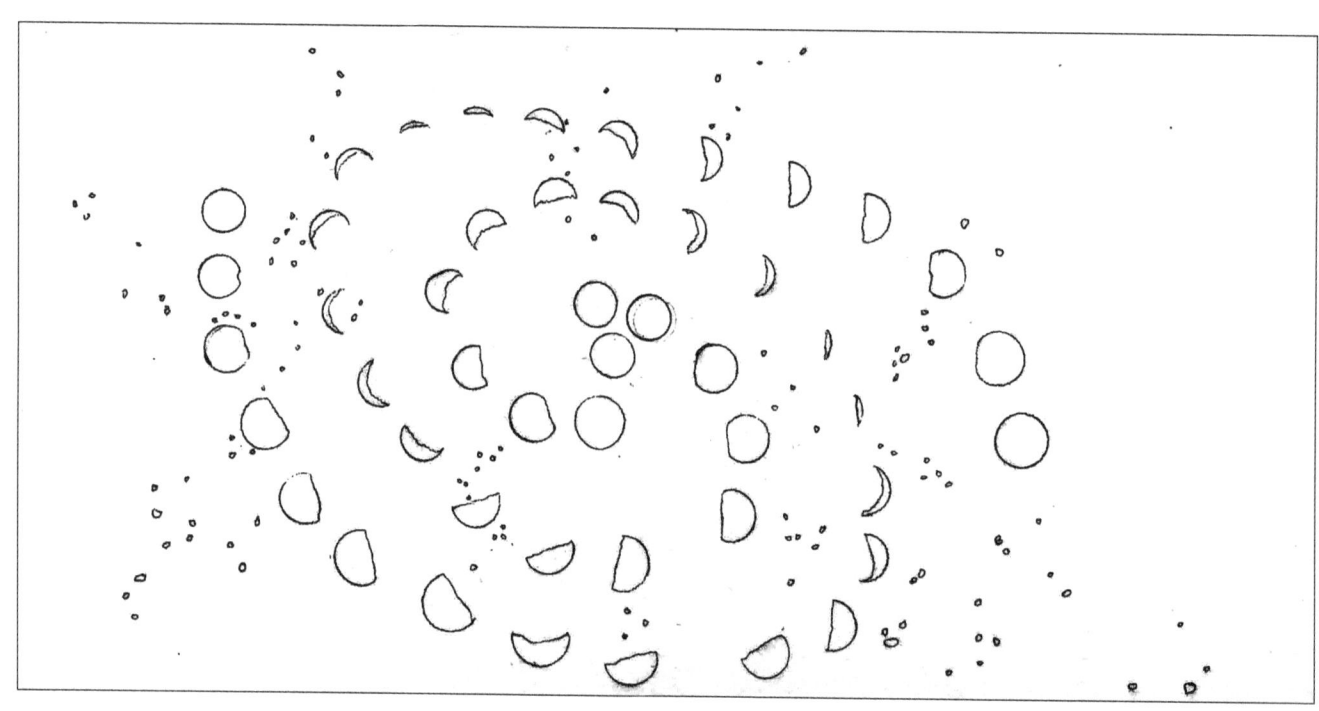

Mussar Avinu:

God said to the Moon: "Go, and the Jewish people will reckon days and years by you." She said to God: "It is impossible for them not to reckon seasons by day also, since it is written, 'And they will be for signs and for set times and for days and years'" (Genesis 1:14).

Torat Imeinu:

God said to the Moon: "Go, and the Jewish people will reckon days and years by you (Genesis 1:14). True, they will also count the days of their lives and mark the longer seasonal passages of the Sun, numbering their work days and the seasons for planting, nurturing, harvesting, and laying fallow.

"By tracking your waxing and waning, however, they will count the evenings that guide them into Shabbat and holiday. By your Sabbaths will they learn Torah, and by your months will they mark the festivals, watching for the New Moon or the Full Moon to give meaning to their life's process through time."

"Ah, then," sighed the Moon, "by the Sun will they count the order of things; by the Moon will they discover the meaning of their days."

Mussar Avinu:

"Go, and holy people will be named after you: Small Jacob [see Amos 7:2], Small Sh'muel [a sage of the Talmud], Small David [see I Samuel 17:14]."

Torat Imeinu:

"O Holy One," said the Moon, "all forms of being express themselves in unending images of Your glory. Small and large alike are made in Your image. The larger Sun and the smaller Moon both reveal the endless diversity of your world."

And God rested in that thought (Genesis 2:2). And God pulsed with the *tzorech ga'voha,* the supernal need for unlimited Being, unlimited possibility. And God knew the fullness of creation, of life, and death, and of *gilgul nefesh,* the cycles of soul passages in this world and the World that is Coming. And God knew that during their embodied passages, human beings would stumble before pain and loss, suffering and death.

As human consciousness evolved into embodied life after Eden, God knew that human beings would experience their world as broken. Some of their explanations of this brokenness would breed terror and fear. Above all, they would need reassuring signs of creation's essential wholeness. They would need a way to find safety in darkness and in light.

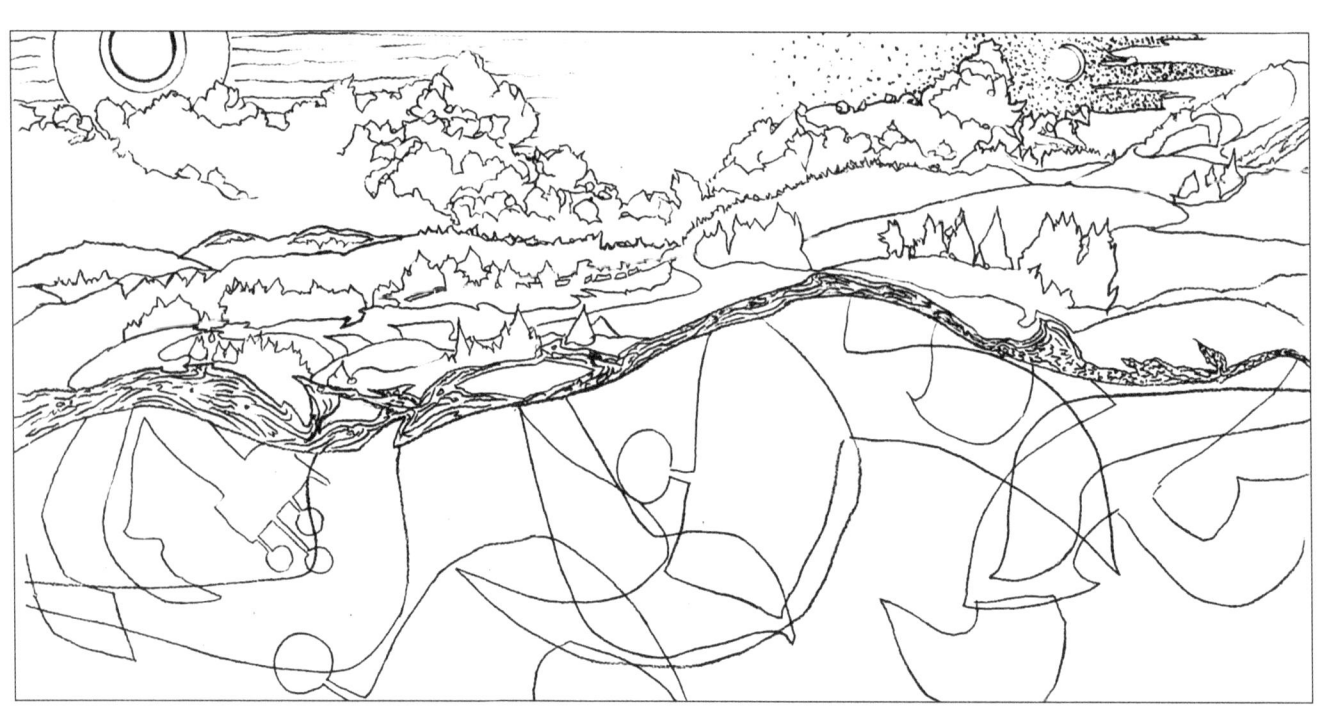

Mussar Avinu:

Seeing that she had not been appeased, the Blessed Holy One said [to the Jewish people]: "Bring an atonement offering for Me, because I made the Moon smaller." This agrees with what Rabbi Shim'on ben Lakish said: "Why is the goat of the New Moon distinguished, in that the Torah says about it, 'For HaShem'? The Blessed Holy One said: 'This goat will be an atonement offering for Me, because I made the moon smaller.'"

Torat Imeinu:

The Blessed Holy One said: "I assigned the Moon to be of smaller physical size than the Sun, which some will misunderstand as a diminishment of the *Shekhinah*. I therefore command the Jewish people to anticipate the New Moon with prayer and ritual, to mark its promise of rebirth and renewal. At the approach of each New Moon, they are to observe a Yom Kippur Katan—a time of at-one-ment and repair for them and for Me. This will draw Me and human beings closer in love and peace, in shared understanding that Moon and Sun serve My Will equally under the same Crown, along with every other element of Being."

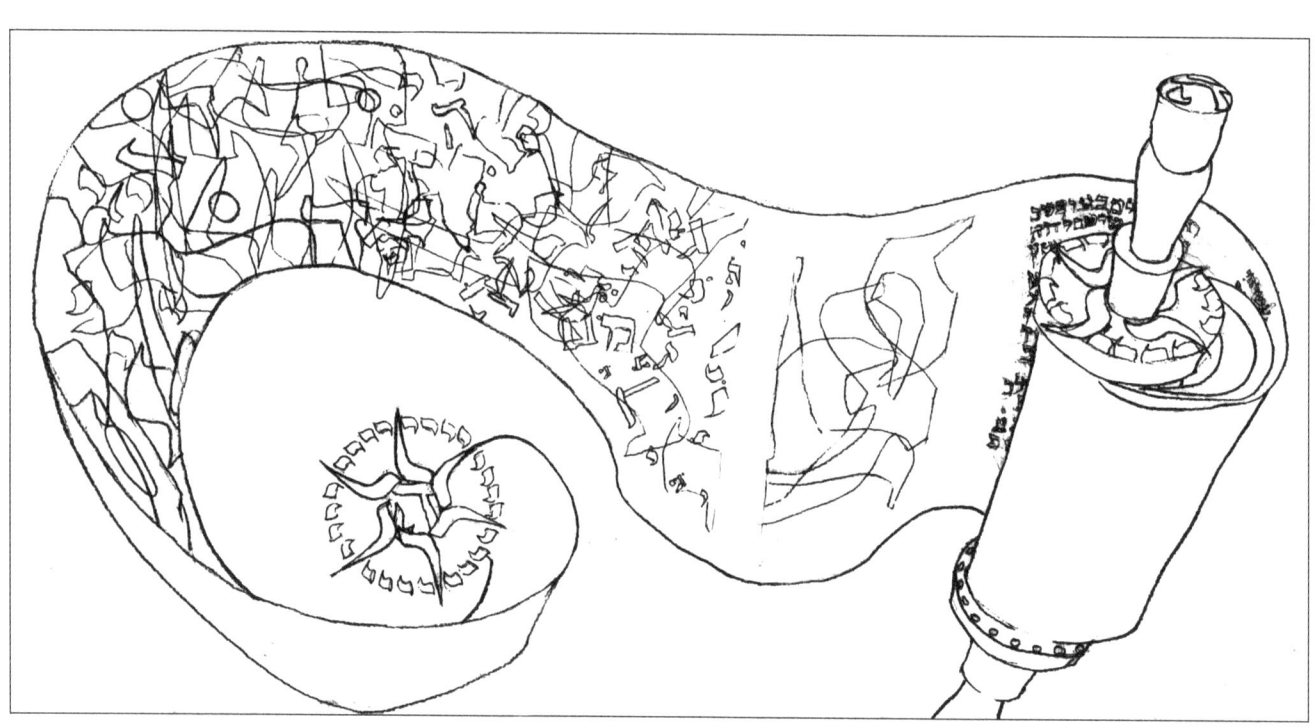

Torat Imeinu:

And the Moon and the Sun bowed beneath the Crown, in awe of the words of Covenant, which bind God as well as human beings.

And they said as one voice: "By Your Wisdom, in words of Torah, will your children discern how to live with the full range of possible experience. They will love You for binding Yourself to them in Covenant. They will call Your Name 'Good.' And, they will call themselves Yisrael, God-wrestlers, struggling in love to accept the entirety of life, including its joys and trials."

They sang together: "Blessed are You, Yah, who gives life to the dead, ensouling all Being, Moon-cycle after Sun-cycle after Moon-cycle . . ."

Notes

Page 5

Resh Lakish said: Cited in Daniel C. Matt, tr. and commentary, *The Zohar* v. 1 (Stanford, CA: Stanford University Press, 2004), p. 58, note 416.

Page 10

. . . this mindset's pernicious effects: "L'shem yichud: For the Sake of Divine Unity," Sarah Stein, Ph.D. and Rabbi Raachel Nathan Jurovics, Ph.D., http://www.tikkun.org/rabbi_lerner/news_item.2006-06-26.1959734093.

Page 19

Birthing the genesis: *Eitz chayim hi*, She is a tree of life (Proverbs 3:18). In poetic language, the mystical tradition sometimes imagines Torah as a woman with whom we are intimately involved in our learning and observance or depicts Torah scholars as husbands or lovers of the *Shekhinah* Herself.

Please note, otherwise unattributed translations are Rabbi Jurovics' work.

So, too, the Holy Blessed One looked into the Torah and created the world: *Midrash Bereshit Rabbah* 1:1. Jewish interpretive practice axiomatically accepts the potential to find meaning even in the spaces between letters on the Torah scroll (and in other sacred text). Innovative insights and alternative holy voices arise from within the "white spaces" surrounding the black-letter text. Rabbi Zalman Schachter-Shalomi derives from a teaching of Reb Levi Yitzhak of Berdichev the insight that the white spaces express the "new Torah" of the Divine Feminine. See *A Merciful God* (Boulder, CO: Albion-Andalus, 2010), pp. 82-8.

Page 20

. . . sacred instruction comes to us in a chorus of voices, masculine, feminine, and non-gendered alike, in accord with Torah's primordial paradigm: While the concept of Torah as expressed through all forms of being is not our subject, just for two examples, please note (1) how the Noahide covenant was established between God and Noah "and every living creature that is with you, for everlasting generations" (Genesis, 9:12), suggesting that non-human life-forms participate in divine covenant; and (2), the teaching in *Midrash Ecclesiastes Rabbah* §4 on Ecclesiastes 1:4, that attributes the earth's endurance to its abiding by God's commandments. See Rabbi David E. Stein, *A Garden of Choice Fruit* (Wyncote, PA: Shomrei Adamah, 1991), p. 53.

We learn Oral Torah from the indwelling divine presence, the *Shekhinah* Herself. See, for example, Rabbi Tirzah Firestone, *The Receiving: Reclaiming Jewish Women's Wisdom* (NY: HarperCollins, 2003); Rabbi Leah Novick, *On the Wings of Shekhinah* (Wheaton, IL: Quest Books, 2008).

Oral Torah comprises divine revelation given along with the Written Torah at Mt. Sinai, discerned through the wisdom of scholars and legal decisors in the unfolding of historical time, a flexible, evolutionary system for responding to changing circumstances in conversation with a fixed sacred text.

Traditionally, the heavenly voice of direct revelation is often called *Bat Kol* (lit., "daughter of a voice"). Regarding *Shekhinah* and Oral Torah, Daniel Matt, ed., *Zohar: The Book of Enlightenment* (Mahwah, NJ: Paulist Press, 1983), p. 206.

Torah poses infinite questions: Interestingly, neither Sun nor Moon are named at this point in the first Genesis creation narrative (although the stars are noted), perhaps to avoid reminding us of the origin stories of peoples who worship Sun and Moon.

. . . the dark side of the Moon: See Sarah Schneider, *Kabbalistic Writings on the Nature of Masculine and Feminine* (Northvale, NJ: Jason Aronson Inc., 2001), pp. 51, 139.

PAGE 21

. . . how do evil and suffering find a place in a universe created by a good and omnipotent God?: For example, see ibid., passim.

". . . there is *no-thing* besides God": Deuteronomy 4:35.

" . . . I create *shalom* (wholeness, wellbeing) and I fashion evil (what we experience as woe)": Isaiah 45:7.

***Tractate Chullin* 60b in the Babylonian Talmud:** Evil, in this sense, refers generally to the question of why creation would include within its possibilities all that we experience as suffering; why would a good God permit that? In terms of personal behavior, however, Jewish tradition puts primary weight on the free will accorded to human beings, while also acknowledging that some positive outcomes arise from free choice that expresses less-than-the-purest motives. For example:

Everything is forseen, yet freedom of choice is given; and the world is judged by grace, yet all is according to the amount of the work (*Avot* 3:19).

R. Samuel Bar Nahman said: The words "Behold, it was good" refer to the impulse to good, and the words "Behold it was very good" (Genesis 1:31) refer to the impulse to evil. But how can the impulse to evil be termed "very good"? Because Scripture teaches that were it not for the impulse to evil, a man would not build a house, take a wife, beget children, or engage in commerce. All such activities come, as Solomon noted, "from a man's rivalry with his neighbor" (Ecclesiastes 4:4). See *Genesis Rabbah* 9:7; *Ecclesiastes Rabbah* 3:11 §3.

R. Hanina b. Papa said: If the *yetzer* (evil inclination) comes and would jest with you, drive it away with words of Torah; and if you would say, "it is not in my power to do so," then the Scripture says, "In yourself should be your trust" (Isaiah 26:3), and remember that God wrote for you the words of the Law, "The desire of the evil *yetzer* is to rule over you, but you are to rule over it" (Genesis 4:7). See *Genesis Rabbah* 22:6; *BT Sukkot* 52a.

Rabbi Hanina said: Everything is in the hands of heaven except for the fear of heaven (i.e., awe, reverence), as it says, "And now, Israel, what does the Lord your God require of you but to fear" (Deuteronomy 10:12). Is the fear of heaven such a little thing? Has not Rabbi Hanina said in the name of Rabbi Shimon Bar Yochai: The Holy Blessed One has in God's treasury nothing except a store of the fear of heaven, as it says, "the fear of the Lord is his treasure" (Isaiah 33:6). See *BT Brachot* 33b.

". . . female and male equally expressive of God's own image": See Genesis 1:27.

PAGE 22

When "woman" becomes shorthand for evil and suffering: How else shall we understand "woman," the feminine archetype, when she is depicted as "both the seductress who lures men into sin and the selfless nurturer who is a crown to her husband"? (Schneider, ibid., p. 178.) When the female archetype bears the burden of redemptive transformation in the universe while stripped of power and dependent on the masculine to facilitate her restoration, how can embodied women be respected as equal partners in *tikkun olam*, in the redemptive partnership between God and humanity?

. . . alternative explanations can surely be imagined: For example, the elegant Lurianic conception of *shevirat ha-kelim* (the shattering of the vessels) during creation can be interpreted so as to explain theodicy without relying on a gendered distribution of qualities. (See Matt, *The Zohar*, v. 1, p. 171, note 506.)

. . . open up less hierarchical understandings: For citations and explication, Rabbi Daniel Siegel, "Moon: White Sliver of *Shekhinah's* Return," *Worlds of Jewish Prayer*, eds. Shohama Harris-Wiener and Jonathan Omer-Man (1993), pp. 231-255.

PAGE 23

. . . the feminine (including the Divine Feminine) has come to be viewed as lesser, as impure, as needing restoration: E.g., consider the need to cleanse and prepare the *Shekhinah*, the Sabbath Bride, from all that besmirches her during the week's accumulation of sin and transgression so that she is fit to mate with

HaKadosh Boruch Hu, an expression of masculine divine qualities. See, for example, R. Elliot Ginsburg, *The Sabbath in the Classical Kabbalah* (Albany, NY: SUNY Press, 1989).

. . . speaking Torah from out of the holy white space where the two big lights were transformed in response to *tzorech ga'voha*: In Kabbalistic thought, a supernal need that can be filled by our performing *mitzvot* (the commandments) with the proper *kavannah* (intention). A spiritual mechanism by which our actions can respond to needs of the Holy One who responds in love to our needs; an aspect of our complete interconnectedness with the Divine.

PAGE 29

Chullin 60b in Two Voices: The citation of *Mussar Avinu* includes the entire text of the relevant passage from *BT Chullin* 60b. In re-imagining what might be found in the white space between the two parts of Genesis 1:16, we engage in what Reb Zalman Schachter-Shalomi calls "participatory epistemology," that is, as we ourselves find our being within the mystical system of the *sephirot* and the Four Worlds, our insights create and validate the unlimited potentialities discoverable in our source texts. (Private conversation, July 2008)

PAGE 31

Mai "gadol"?: See *BT Shabbat* 21b: *Mai Chanukah*? "What is Chanukah all about?"—so, "what is 'big' all about?" The Hebrew words *gadol* (big) and *katan* (small) commonly relate to size and, by extension, to importance. For example, each of these adjectives yields a noun: *gadlut* (the quality of greatness, expansiveness) and *katnut* (the quality of limitation, constraint).

According to the first half of Genesis 1:16, both luminaries express the quality of *gadlut*, both are *gadol*. In the second part of the verse, the *Chullin* text reads *katan* as diminished, subverting the possibility of understanding the moon as physically smaller while remaining equal in function, purpose, and power.

Rabbi Daniel Siegel writes, commenting on *Zohar Bereishit* 20b: "Here, what was latent is now manifest. Each body was a light unto itself, and the moon is no less for having been 'diminished.' The lights that have descended into our reality, particularly the qualities of *Binah, Tiferet,* and *Malkhut* (*sephirot* usually associated with the feminine) have not in reality separated from the 'higher' masculine qualities but are rejoined, and indeed each is included in the other." See ibid., p. 244.

The goal of our new *midrash*, then, is to consider what it would mean if we imagined Moon and Sun as equal from the beginning, without waiting for the Moon's equal nature to be revealed or restored over time.

. . . the Divine Will looked into Torah: See, for example, the well-known *midrash* concerning Torah as the divine model of creation in *Bereshit Rabbah* 1:1; see also Proverbs 8:22-31 concerning the role of Wisdom/*Shekhinah* in the design and implementation of creation.

. . . an alternation of evening and morning: The Holy One rolls light before darkness and darkness before light . . . and separates between day and night (*Ha'ma'ariv aravim*, from the evening liturgy).

PAGE 35

It is possible: The Hebrew sentence "*efshar lisnei m'lachim she'yishtamshu b'keter echad*" may be read either as question or statement: "is it possible for two sovereigns to rule under one crown?" or "it is possible for two sovereigns to rule under one crown."

. . . the Crown: At the top of the Kabbalistic Tree of Life, which depicts the mysterious interconnection of attributes within the Divine Being, sits *Keter* (Crown), also known as Will/Desire. *Chochmah* (Knowledge of the Entirety) and *Binah* (Capacity to Discern Variety) are understood as the pair of attributes immediately under the Crown that manifest divine generativity, creativity, and power. (See illustration on pages 56-57.)

The Crown sits above the other emanations of divinity: As, for example, the Holy One "orders the orbits of a sky full of stars, *u'm'sader et ha-kochavim b'mishm'roteihem ba-rakiah kir'tzono*" (*Ha'ma'ariv aravim*, from the evening liturgy).

Partner me with my beloved: "The darkness is a love-tent for the sun" (Psalm 19:5b-6a; tr. R. Zalman Schachter-Shalomi, *Siddur Kol Koreh* [ALEPH: Philadelphia, PA, 1999], § II, p. 1).

Without respite from its glare: "The sun now rises, like groom from bride of night, like a joyous runner, trembling to start the race. From one end of the heavens climbing into the sky, arcing to the horizon, where sun sets into night, nothing can hide from its light" (Psalm 19:6-7; tr. R. Zalman Schachter-Shalomi, ibid., p. 2). Overpowering light, like darkness, can blind us to the amazingly differentiated glory of Creation; perhaps it is in shade and moonlight that we find our fullest appreciation of a world filled with the Divine Presence (see Isaiah 6:3).

In the modulation between the Sun's light and mine: *Ezer k'negdo*, a helpmeet opposite: the intentional and mutually essential tension between the Sun's gravitational stability and the

Moon's transformative waxing and waning. This same term is applied to Adam and Eve (Genesis 2:18). The alternation of night and day permits germination and invites the inspiration of dreamtime. The "half-way point" between evening and morning, *chatzot ha'laila*, represents an especially propitious moment for devotional prayer.

Note also, in the morning praise for God's creation of the heavenly lights, this attribution of consciousness and will to the heavenly bodies: "The stars and the planets You made to give light. You formed them all conscious, all worthy and wise. Knowledge and power You gave them to shine. Like powerful assistants, they serve You in space" (tr. Rabbi Zalman Schachter-Shalomi in *The P'nai Or Siddur for Shabbat Morning*, Rabbi Marcia Prager, p. 19).

. . . from *gilgul* to *gilgul*: Reincarnation is included among Jewish teachings on the immortality of the soul, in some instances positing the recycling of souls through as many embodiments as necessary for each soul to complete the mission it accepted upon its first incarnation. Some interpreters even suggest that souls may make a sort of bodhisattva choice to return after their initial mission has been completed in order to help another soul. For overviews of the range of Jewish teachings on the afterlife, *What Happens after I Die* by Rifat Soncino and Daniel B. Syme (NY: URJ Press, 1990); *Does the Soul Survive* by Elie Kaplan Spitz (Woodstock, VT: Jewish Lights Publishing, 2000); and *Jewish Views of the Afterlife* by Simcha Paull Raphael (Northvale, NJ: Jason Aronson Inc., 1996; second edition, Lanham: Rowman & Littlefield Publishers, 2019).

According to some Torah commentators, we may account death as one of the good things God created. For example, a *midrash* relates that the Torah scroll of Rabbi Meir had a textual variant near the conclusion of the creation story: "And God saw everything that God had made and behold it was very good" (Genesis 1:31). What was it that God, seeing all of creation, beheld to be very good? It was death. Rabbi Meir's version read *ve-hinneh tov mavet*, and behold, good is death (*Genesis Rabbah* 9:5).

PAGE 39

"What importance does that have? What use is a lamp in daylight?": As the dialogue continues in *Chullin* 60b, God offers various arguments in order to placate the Moon for the divine command to diminish herself. By the end of the passage, God is depicted as asking Israel to bring an atonement offering for the divine transgression of diminishing the Moon. Clearly, this ancient text holds within itself an implicit recognition of the injustice done to the Moon, who merits honor equal to that of the Sun.

PAGE 43

. . . to give meaning to their life's process through time: The Jewish calendar keeps time according to solar-adjusted lunar calculations, so that holy days and festivals remain in their appropriate season. Specific Torah portions are assigned to each week. In the Jewish way of keeping time, the evening marks the beginning of a new day and the significance of each daytime is determined by the nature of the evening that precedes it, as in the difference between Shabbat time and the work-days of the week (which end at sundown on Friday). Note Isaiah 66:23: "And from new moon to new moon, and from Sabbath to Sabbath—says the Eternal One—all flesh shall come to worship Me."

Page 47

Small and large alike are made in Your image: We may well wonder to or with whom God is speaking in the first creation narrative: "*na'aseh b'tzalmenu*, let us make [an] 'adam' (an earthling) in our image," Genesis 1:26. Some commentators consider "let us" as a sort of royal we; others imagine Divinity consulting with the angelic hosts. Perhaps, if we consider Divinity the sole source of all being, we may imagine God addressing the intention to manifest human beings to the previously manifested elements of the cosmos; if we, along with the entirety of the cosmos, derive our nature from the one source, then we are bound in mutuality of concern and responsibility to every other form of being.

And God rested in that thought (Genesis 2:2): ". . . the personal growth and education of the Creator, the true subject of all biblical myth," Rabbi Arthur Green, *Radical Judaism* (New Haven and London: Yale University Press, 2010), p. 43. Genesis 2:2: "And God rested on the seventh day from all the work which God had made."

. . . the World that is Coming: In Hebrew, both the afterlife and the messianic age are referred to as *Olam Ha-Ba* (the World to Come or the World that is Coming). This overlap in terminology links the soul in its immortality to our day-by-day evolution toward ever higher states of spiritual, emotional, intellectual, and practical capabilities—our evolution toward "redeemed time" for all being on our planet and in the cosmos. Jewish mystical teachings often underscore the interconnectedness of present reality and emergent redemption. In some cases, the divine quality of *Binah* is identified with the world that is coming (e.g., Matt, *Zohar*, v. 1, p. 39).

As human consciousness evolved into embodied life after Eden: See, for example, Genesis 3:8-24, concerning the expulsion from Eden into a world that would not yield its bounty without strenuous labor. The Zohar relates that Adam and Eve did not manifest as material beings until after leaving the garden:

> As soon as he was driven from the Garden of Eden and had need of forms suited to this world, "the Lord God," Scripture says, "made for Adam and for his wife garments of skin (*'or*) and clothed them" (*Bereishit* 3:21). Formerly they were garments of light (*or*), to wit, of the celestial light in which Adam ministered in the Garden of Eden. For, inasmuch as it is the resplendency of the celestial light that ministers in the Garden of Eden, when first man entered into the Garden, the Holy One, blessed be He, clothed him first in the raiment of that light. Otherwise he could not have entered there. When driven out, however, he had need of other garments; hence "garments of skin" (*Zohar Shemot,* London: Soncino, 1934, § 2, 229b).

Biblical commentator Avivah Gottlieb Zornberg emphasizes the strand of interpretation that finds opportunity in the expulsion into our difficult and complex world:

> In the biblical narrative, however, the vertical imagery of falling is entirely absent. Instead, an *outward* movement expels Adam and Eve from the Garden: "And

the Lord God *banished* him from the Garden of Eden. . . . He *drove* the man *out*" (Genesis 3:23-24). This is not a fall but, in a sense, a birth. Paradise is lost, but a larger, if more agitated life looms. See *The Murmuring Deep: Reflections on the Biblical Unconscious* (NY: Schocken Books, 2009), p. 17.

Rabbi Sylvia Rothschild offers a related teaching on Genesis on the Leo Baeck College website (lbc.ac.uk), September 24, 2013:

> The story of the leaving of Eden is not a tragic event, something that should never have happened; and we should not spend our lives yearning to return there—after all, why would God create a garden in which there are two trees that we should not eat from, if not to challenge us and to provide a catalyst?
>
> Adam and Eve in the garden are innocents, they are like newborn children, and if kept in that state they will never be able to grow and learn and develop their own ideas and identities. Making mistakes is part of growing up and becoming who we are. The story of leaving the Garden of Eden is a story of maturation, of acquiring independence, of leaving home in order to become one's own full self. Making mistakes is how we learn.

. . . signs of creation's essential wholeness: See again Isaiah 45:7, "I form light and create darkness; I create shalom (wholeness, wellbeing) and I fashion evil (what we experience as woe)." The Divine Will requires that everything be possible, even that which we experience as evil.

Page 51

Bring an atonement offering for Me: See Numbers 28:15. The Biblical Hebrew term usually translated as sacrifice is *korban*, based on the root letters for nouns and verbs related to "drawing near." Offerings brought to God were essentially a means of drawing closer, in times of gratitude, petition, and reconciliation, not a matter of giving something up—offerings enacted the human and divine desire to remain in balanced relationship.

At the approach of each New Moon: Jewish practice includes recognizing each New Moon as a women's festival, and the eve of the New Moon as a Yom Kippur Kattan (a "little day of atonement"), an opportunity to review one's behavior over the past month with an eye to spiritual refinement. See "Yom Kippur Kattan and the Cycles of T'shuvah: Teachings of R. Zalman Schachter-Shalomi" (Philadelphia, PA: ALEPH, 1999).

Page 55

And the Moon and the Sun bowed beneath the Crown: One way to understand the *mitzvot*/commandments is as God's revelation to humankind of how we are to fulfill the Divine Will to love God and to love one another. It is by the commandments that we most fully live: Leviticus 18:5, "*v'chai bahem*," that you may live by [the *mitzvot*]. According to rabbinic tradition, God observes the commandments as we do, e.g., God puts on light as if it were a *tallit*/prayer shawl, prays, studies Torah. See *BT Rosh haShanah* 17b, *Berachot* 6a. Jewish tradition demonstrates comfort with the notion that Divinity itself learns and evolves. See, for example, R. Yehudah's teaching that God studies the Torah for the first three hours of every day in *BT Avodah Zarah* 3b or *Babba Metziah* 59b, where God rejoices that human expositors of Torah have accepted the responsibility for its meaning, in effect, learning with and from human beings.

They will call Your Name 'Good.': "*Hatov shimcha*, Your Name is Good," closing verse of the next-to-last section of the *Amidah* (a series of prayers central to Jewish liturgy), comprising a litany of the continual blessings Divinity bestows on us.

. . . to accept the entirety of life, including its trials: Job 2:10, "Should we accept only good from God and not accept evil?"

"Blessed are You, Yah, who gives life to the dead": Closing verse of the second section of the *Amidah,* which reminds us of the cycling and recycling of life out of death, of the fecundity of endless life rolling from dark to light.

BIOGRAPHIES

DR. SARAH STEIN

Sarah is an Associate Professor of Media Studies at North Carolina State University, with a background in documentary film-making, including winning an Oscar for film editing. She is ordained as a contemplative minister through the Interfaith Theological Seminary and has worked as a Spiritual Director for twenty years. Her interests encompass feminist revisions of theological texts and received understandings of common religious themes.

RABBI DR. RAACHEL JUROVICS

Reb Raachel earned B.A., M.A., and Ph.D. degrees in English Medieval Literature from UCLA. She has served in numerous community and congregational leadership capacities, with an emphasis on human rights issues. Ordained in 2003 by the Jewish Renewal Seminary, she will complete her service as President of OHALAH, the Association of Rabbis and Cantors for Jewish Renewal, in January 2020. Reb Raachel is the founding spiritual leader of Yavneh: A Jewish Renewal Community in Raleigh, North Carolina, and maintains a multi-faith spiritual direction practice.

Mary Blocher

Mary understands herself as innately four things—a Texan woman, a veteran, a spouse, and Jewish. Her mother raised her to reject the automatic exclusion of women from anything. The United States Army taught her to appreciate the rights and liberties we should all express in our lives. She and her husband Joe met in the Army and continue to explore life-long partnership and love. Converting to Judaism after a decade of searching for her faith, Mary joyfully accepts the daily challenge to live in Covenant with YHVH.

Andrea Gomez

Andrea received her B.F.A. in painting in 1972 from the Tyler School of Art, Temple University, where she not only studied painting and drawing in all its forms, but also apprenticed as an animator. She made independent experimental animation from 1972 to the mid-1980s, accruing various awards and honors, including being chosen an AFI fellow.

Returning to painting in 1988, she opened a studio in Artspace, Raleigh, North Carolina, where her work was acknowledged in numerous newspaper reviews, shows, awards, and collection inclusions.

Leaving Artspace in 2001, Andrea built her own studio. Her work reflects wide interests in subject matter, mastery of many media, and often reflects Biblical or theological themes. Her portraits are prized for their presentation of the subject's personality and biography through facial expression, posture and *mise en scene*, giving lively voice to her subject's personal narratives. (Please visit her website at www.gomezart.net.)

www.ingramcontent.com/pod-product-compliance
Lightning Source LLC
Chambersburg PA
CBHW041153230426
43673CB00036B/508